The World of Inventions

Duncan Searl

Globe
Fearon

Upper Saddle River, New Jersey
www.globefearon.com

Project Editor: Kim Choi
Supervising Editor: Lynn W. Kloss
Production Editor: Amy Benefiel
Senior Designer: Janice Noto-Helmers
Electronic Page Production: Jeffrey Engel
Editorial Assistant: Jennifer Watts

ISBN 0-130-23758-2

Printed in the United States of America
1 2 3 4 5 6 7 8 9 10   04 03 02 01 00

1-800-848-9500
www.globefearon.com

Contents

Introduction

People have always looked for ways to make life easier and better. As a result, we live in homes, not in caves. We can travel long distances in cars, trains, and airplanes. Over the centuries, we have also improved the ways we **communicate**. Communication means all the ways we send information, thoughts, ideas, and feelings from one person to another. We communicate mostly with words, sounds, and pictures.

Today, we can send and receive messages instantly. We can send e-mail around the world in a second. We can watch history being made on TV. We can enjoy a variety of books, movies, and music. Even simple tools such as ballpoint pens have improved our ability to communicate.

In this book, you will learn about important **inventions**, new ideas and machines, that have helped people to communicate. You will see how each invention created new knowledge. You will see how that knowledge then led to new inventions.

Some inventions came from one person's work. Others were the result of teams of people working together. Many inventions happened by accident. Others appeared in different parts of the world at the same time.

Inventors are still changing the ways we communicate. They are doing it a fast rate, too. Right now, inventors are working on new ideas. Some of those ideas are sure to change our lives.

Chapter One
Putting Words on Paper

Our world is full of books and magazines. Libraries and bookstores have dozens of books on every topic. That was not always true, though. For thousands of years, inventors have worked hard to make the printed word part of our lives.

Clay Tablets

More than 6,000 years ago, books were tablets of clay. Writers used sticks to press words into the soft clay. Clay books were heavy and hard to read. They broke easily. They also took up a lot of space.

Many early clay tablets from Sumeria were records showing who owned pieces of land.

A Piece of Papyrus

By 3500 B.C., the Egyptians had found a better writing material—**papyrus**. Reeds called papyrus grow along the Nile River. The Egyptians cut the reeds into strips. Then they soaked them and hammered them flat. When the papyrus reeds dried, a thin sheet of writing material was formed. From the word *papyrus*, the English language gets the word *paper*.

The ancient Egyptians wrote on papyrus, using brushes and inks made from minerals.

For thousands of years, people all over the world used papyrus. However, papyrus reeds grow only in Egypt. In ancient times, getting the reeds was difficult. People needed a writing material that they could get more easily.

Animal Skins

One solution to the problem of finding a writing material was **parchment**. Parchment came from animal skins. To make it, people first soaked the skins. Then they rubbed the skins until they were perfectly smooth. Next, workers sewed the sheets of parchment together. Finally, they added a wooden or leather cover to protect the sheets. These were the first books.

During the Middle Ages, monks in Europe copied texts onto parchment. They wrote with quills, which are long, stiff feathers. Often, these books were very beautiful. The monks decorated the books with gold and silver and with painted designs. This meant that copying a single book could take a year or longer!

Papermaking

In ancient China, people made books from rolls of silk or bamboo. The Chinese used the same brush for writing and painting. Their books often combined words and pictures.

In the Middle Ages, monks in Europe used parchment to make books.

Around the year A.D. 50, the Chinese invented paper. To make it, they boiled old rags and ropes to form a liquid called pulp. Then they spread the pulp out on a screen of bamboo. When the pulp dried, it formed a thin sheet of fibers. This was the first paper.

The news about paper traveled west slowly. By A.D. 800, Arabs in the Middle East were making paper. Many Arab cities were centers of learning. Papermakers helped teachers spread their knowledge. In ancient Baghdad, there were scribes. These were people who copied books for sale.

Printing Blocks

It was hard work to copy a book. A scribe could spend years on each book. These books were very expensive. They also had many mistakes. There had to be a better way.

By the 800s, the Chinese had a new idea. They used printing blocks. First, they carved the text for a page into a wooden block. Next, they coated the block with ink. Then they pressed the block onto paper. They could print many copies of a page this way.

Printing with wooden blocks was fine for short works. Carving the blocks for a whole book, however, took months. Often, the carved words were not clear, either. The blocks soon cracked and warped. To make better books, printers needed a new invention.

Movable Type

Around the year 1450, a German named Johann Gutenberg had an idea. Why not place each letter of the alphabet on a separate piece of metal? These pieces of metal, called **type**, could be moved around to form different words.

Actually, Gutenberg was not the first to have this idea. Two hundred years earlier, Korean inventors had made movable type. However, news about the Asian invention had never reached Europe.

Gutenberg built the first **printing press**. The press used a wooden screw to press paper onto type. He also made special ink. He spread the ink on the type. In 1456, Gutenberg printed his first book, the *Bible.*

Printing presses changed the world. Suddenly, there were many more books. Information could now spread quickly. People became hungry for knowledge. They began to question old ideas. A new period of learning began.

Writing Machines

Printing presses changed the way people made books. In offices, however, workers still had to write by hand. Many people tried to build a writing machine. In 1873, one of them finally succeeded.

The printing press made books available to more people than ever before. It helped spread new ideas quickly.

Christopher Sholes named his invention the "literary piano." Others called it the typewriter. Soon, there were typewriters in offices around the world.

Instant Copies

Every day, office workers quickly copy all kinds of documents. They can send these papers instantly to places around the world. A hundred years ago, few people dreamed of communicating so easily and quickly.

Photocopiers were invented in the early 1900s. Office workers did not like the machines, though. Early photocopiers used wet chemicals and film that were very messy.

One office worker found a better way. In 1938, he invented a "dry" photocopier. It used plain paper, not film. These machines were a big success.

Before photocopiers became common, typists could make just a few copies of their work. To make a copy, they had to use a messy sheet of carbon paper. They put the carbon paper into their typewriters as they typed. The copies were not very good. There was no easy way to copy documents, drawings, photographs, or pages from books. Think of all the ways people depend on photocopiers today. Photocopiers let us pass on information quickly and easily.

Along with photocopiers, the fax machine is also changing the way we communicate. This important machine did not become common until the 1970s.

In 1895, a German scientist invented a new electric cell. It could "see" light and dark areas on paper. Some newspapers used this machine to send pictures over a wire.

More than 70 years passed. Finally, people put the machine to work in a big way. It became the fax machine!

QWERTY

Look at a computer keyboard. The first six letters in the top row of letters are Q, W, E, R, T, and Y. Have you ever wondered why?

When Christopher Sholes invented the typewriter, he put the letters in alphabetical order. This caused a problem, though. When a typist worked quickly, the keys jammed. Sholes could not figure out how to stop the jamming. So he decided to slow the typist down.

Sholes changed the order of the letters. He put the most common letters far apart. That way, the bars that held those letters would not jam.

This new order was QWERTY. Sholes said it made typing easier. Actually, the opposite was true. With QWERTY, a typist's fingers must cover a much greater distance on the keyboard. Typewriters using QWERTY did not jam. So typists learned the new order.

Later, Sholes improved his typewriter. The keys no longer jammed when they were in alphabetical order. By then, however, typists had learned QWERTY. They did not want to change. Today, in the age of computers, we still use QWERTY. This order is hard to learn and serves no purpose. However, it seems to be too late to change it. Too many people have learned it!

Chapter Two
Getting People Together

The wheel is one of the most important inventions of all. Wheels made modern **transportation** possible. As a result, cities grew. Then people needed better ways to get around. They needed faster ways to communicate when they were apart.

Putting the World on Wheels

The first wheel rolled into history almost 6,000 years ago. It wasn't used for transportation, though. Potters in the Middle East invented the wheel. They turned clay on it. That way, they could shape pots more easily.

Soon, the wheel was putting people in motion. People have found a clay tablet from Iraq that is 5,000 years old. It shows a war chariot pulled by two horses.

For thousands of years, wheels were very heavy. Some were pieces of wood cut from tree trunks. In ancient China, wheels were made of stone.

Change came slowly. People began cutting out sections of the wooden wheels. This made the wheels lighter. Soon, there were wheels with spokes. People also put metal rims around wheels. That made the wheels last longer.

As wheels improved, so did **vehicles**. The ancient Greeks and Romans made faster and lighter chariots. By the Middle Ages, some Europeans traveled in coaches with four wheels. By the early 1800s, **stagecoaches** rattled down U.S. roads.

As wheels improved, so did transportation. Better transportation meant that people could communicate new ideas more quickly.

Wagons and stagecoaches helped people send messages more quickly. Such vehicles carried newspapers, mail, and books. They let people from different cities get together and exchange ideas. Still, these vehicles had a major problem. They could go only as fast as the animals that pulled them.

All Aboard!

In the 1700s, inventors put steam to work. They built engines that turned steam into power. Early **steam engines** pumped water. They also ran machines in factories.

By the 1770s, steam engines were strong enough to pull vehicles on wheels. The railroad was born in the early 1800s. The first trains were carts that carried ore in mines. Before long, though, people wanted a ride.

Railroads allowed people and information to travel quickly.

In the United States, the first passenger train made its first trip in 1831. By 1836, 1,000 miles of railroad tracks linked cities in the eastern United States. By the Civil War, tracks stretched west to the Mississippi River.

Railroads changed life in the United States. Towns and cities sprang up along the tracks. People could ship goods long distances. Mail, newspapers, and books reached readers in record time. People could travel more easily.

As railroads grew, they provided jobs for many people. Some people worked as engineers and conductors. Others laid tracks and sold tickets. The

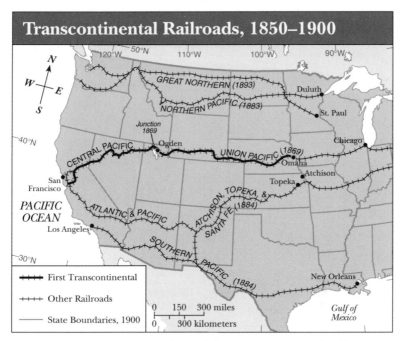

Transcontinental Railroads, 1850–1900

In 1869, workers completed the first transcontinental railroad in the United States. It linked the entire nation, from east to west.

railroads also kept inventors busy. These inventors made switches, signals, brakes, and thousands of other new devices. Railroads were drawing the people of the United States closer together.

Behind the Wheel

By 1900, a web of railroads crossed the United States. Railroads were the best possible way to travel, people thought. Soon, though, a new vehicle roared into their lives. It was the automobile!

The automobile was a group effort. Many people shared their ideas. One man, however, put millions of Americans behind the wheel. His name is Henry Ford.

15

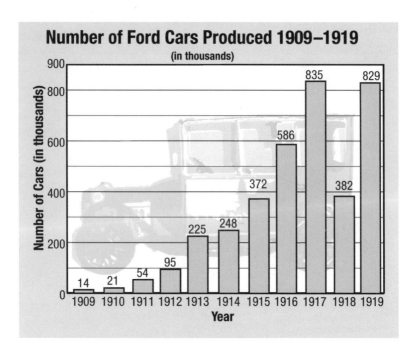

Number of Ford Cars Produced 1909–1919
(in thousands)

Number of Cars (in thousands)

Year	1909	1910	1911	1912	1913	1914	1915	1916	1917	1918	1919
Cars	14	21	54	95	225	248	372	586	835	382	829

In 1908, Henry Ford invented moving assembly lines and put them to use in his factory. Workers in different parts of the factory helped put each car together. Each worker added a new part to the car. Workers in assembly lines could make cars quickly and cheaply.

Over the next 10 years, Ford's factories made millions of cars. All looked exactly the same. "You can have any color car you like, as long as it's black," Ford joked. The assembly line meant serious savings, though. A Ford car cost $780 in 1910. By 1924, it cost only $290.

New businesses sprang up because of cars. Tire companies, gas stations, and car repair shops opened. Workers were hired to pave new roads. Soon, "motor hotels," or motels, became popular. Drive-in movies and drive-through restaurants were next. Cars changed every part of American life. Thanks to Henry Ford, people could now travel long distances more easily to meet with other people across the United States.

Up, Up, and Away

For thousands of years, people had dreamed of flying. Some even strapped on wings and tried to fly off cliffs.

By the 1800s, inventors were using science to solve the mystery of flying. They did experiments with gliders. They built wind tunnels to study how wings worked. Each new discovery brought them closer to the secrets of flight.

Two brothers from Ohio took the final step. Wilbur and Orville Wright repaired bicycles during the day. At night, they dreamed of flying. They studied the designs of airplanes that had failed. They tried to figure out what other builders had done wrong. At last, they built an airplane that could really fly.

In December 1903, Orville Wright took off. His first flight lasted just 12 seconds. It covered only 131 feet of a windy North Carolina beach. Even so, the age of flight had begun.

Wilbur and Orville Wright's invention helped bring the world closer together.

By 1909, a plane could carry people up to 125 miles. During World War I (1914–1918), planes spied on enemy troops. By the 1920s, airplanes affected everyday life. People who could afford to do so flew across the United States in a few hours. An airmail letter traveled around the world in a few days instead of weeks.

Today, airplanes make our world a much smaller place. Planes travel ten times faster than trains. People fly around the world for business meetings. They plan vacations all over the globe. With a plane ticket, the world is yours!

Women on Wheels

In the late 1800s, a simple new invention swept the nation—bicycles. Actually, bikes had been around for a while. The early models, however, had wooden wheels. They did not have pedals or brakes. They were not very popular.

By the 1880s, bicycles had pedals, chains, and brakes. Airfilled rubber tires also gave them a lift. More than 500 factories in the United States turned out the new two-wheelers.

Almost anyone can ride a bicycle. In the United States, almost everyone did. Ten million cyclists took to the roads by 1900. Every town had its own bicycle club. Bicycle races became more popular than baseball!

Bicycles brought freedom and fun to ordinary people, especially to women and children. They were no longer stuck alone at home all day. They could pedal wherever they wanted to go. They could even visit with friends in other towns.

Chapter Three
Recording Sounds

Inventions related to storing or transmitting sound helped people to communicate more effectively. Today, CDs and tapes let us enjoy our favorite music all the time. People listen to books on tape. Radio stations play music from all over the world. Sound is an important part of TV shows and movies, too.

The First Phonograph

In 1875, inventors learned to **record** sound, or store it so that people could listen to it at another time or place. The first machine that could record and play back sound was the **phonograph**. Thomas Edison built the first phonograph in 1877. It took him only a day to make it. The phonograph was a small machine with a simple handle. The handle turned a **cylinder**, or tube, wrapped in foil. As the foil turned, a needle scratched a groove in it.

Edison himself turned the crank. As he did, he shouted the words to a song: "Mary had a little lamb." He then put the needle back at the starting point. He turned the handle again. A scratchy squeak came out of the little machine: "Mary had a little lamb."

Workers in Edison's lab looked on in amazement. The phonograph had just been born. Most inventions are a group effort. Many people work on them. Often, different inventors try to invent the same thing at the same time. The phonograph, however, belonged completely to Thomas Edison. No one else had ever thought of anything like it.

Early phonographs had a giant horn sticking out of them. A person spoke or sang into the horn to make a recording. The horn also made the sounds louder when they were played back. The horn worked well if one person was singing. It didn't do a good job of recording a large group, though.

Thomas Edison was too busy inventing the light bulb to improve his phonograph. So other inventors worked on the idea. Early recordings were too scratchy. People wanted a fuller, more natural sound.

The first recordings were made on cylinders, or metal tubes. They looked like little tin cans. In 1887, flat recording disks called **records** were invented. The sound improved. Inventors also began making "master" recordings on metal disks. From these, many wax copies could be made and sold. The new, improved phonograph was called a gramophone.

Thomas Edison's phonograph was the first invention that could record sounds and play them back.

America Hears the Beat

One hundred years ago, most Americans lived on farms or in small towns. Few had a chance to go to concerts. Many never heard music unless they made it themselves.

When gramophone records became available, music became part of everyday life. People could listen to records in their own homes. They could try out new dances. They could enjoy music from faraway places.

Recorded sound created a huge music industry. More and more musicians could reach large audiences. The quality of recordings quickly improved. Two improvements were the **microphone** and the

21

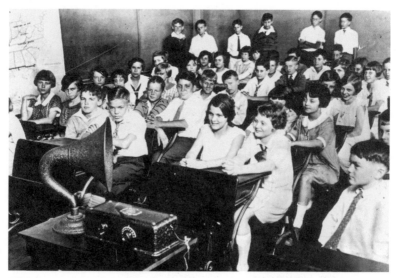

The gramophone allowed people to listen to all kinds of recorded music in their schools and homes.

loudspeaker. These devices had been invented for the telephone in 1878. Soon, inventors put them to work in the phonograph. This happens often: One invention leads to improvements in another.

78s, 33s, and 45s

As they played, early records spun around on a turntable 78 times per minute. So they were called "78s." The records were made from shellac. Shellac is a hard, natural material that is something like plastic.

By 1946, companies began making records from vinyl, a type of plastic. At about the same time, they began making long-playing records.

Long-playing records, or LPs, spun around $33\frac{1}{3}$ times per minute. The "33s" could hold up to half an hour of music on each side. That meant that people could listen to a long piece of music without changing the record.

In the 1950s, small vinyl disks became available. They had a single song on each side. Called "singles" or "45s," they spun around 45 times per minute as they played. The 45s were 7 inches across. Teenagers could carry them to parties and get-togethers.

Until the 1980s, recorded music was sold on records like these.

Going to Tape

Making a record required a studio filled with equipment. People wanted a simpler way to record sound. The invention of **magnetic tape** in the 1930s made the **tape recorder** possible.

With a tape recorder, people could record sound without complex equipment and recording studios.

The new machines had many uses. Scientists could now record the sounds of birds and animals in the wild. News reporters could record speeches and interviews. For the first time, people could even record the voices of their own family and friends.

Early tape recorders, however, needed large reels of tape. Using them could be difficult. In the 1960s, much smaller magnetic tapes became available. They came in little cases, so people started calling these tapes "cassettes."

Cassette tapes were neat and easy to handle. People could buy cassettes with music already recorded on them. They could make their own recordings on blank tapes. In addition, people could listen to cassette tapes at home or in their cars. Portable players allowed joggers to listen to tapes as they ran. Cassette tapes were also used in telephone answering machines.

Compact Disks

By the 1980s, millions of Americans owned expensive phonographs called stereo sound systems. Many families owned dozens of LPs to play on their stereos. All of their favorite music was on vinyl records. Then it happened. A new invention made all of that equipment old-fashioned!

Two groups of scientists invented the **compact disk**, or CD. Some of the scientists worked in Holland. Others were in Japan. Companies in Japan began selling the first compact disks and CD players in 1981.

CDs have tiny bumps and pits on them. You cannot see them without a microscope. When you play a CD, a laser reads the information in the bumps and pits. The laser then sends an electric signal to the speakers.

CDs were an immediate success. Record companies quickly switched to the new format. The small disks are easy to use and store. Only 5 inches across, they hold up to 75 minutes of sound. Unlike records, they do not break or scratch easily.

Imagine Thomas Edison listening to today's cassettes and CDs. How amazed he would be!

Back to the Future

The world's oldest sound recordings date back to the 1880s. At that time, people recorded sound on cylinders of wax. These old cylinders are now in museums. Over the years, however, most of them have shrunk. Some are very weak. Playing the cylinders would damage them. So no one has heard most of them for years.

The cylinders hold a great deal of history, such as speeches by presidents and songs by well-known singers. Often, the cylinders are the only recordings these people made. The cylinders also hold oral histories. Many people recorded their memories of the Civil War and other major events on wax cylinders. The photo shows a museum curator examining some wax cylinders.

We learn about history mostly from writing and pictures. Voices from the past, however, are often very powerful. They give us a vivid impression of what people and events were really like.

In the year 2000, scientists found a new way to listen to these old recordings. They invented a laser that could "read" the grooves in the wax and make modern recordings of them on CDs. The world's oldest recordings now have a new life.

Chapter Four
Capturing the Image

Have you ever noticed that there are no photographs of Christopher Columbus or George Washington? Why not? The reason is that **photography** was not invented until the 1830s. That is when people began to capture images, or pictures, on metal, glass, and then paper.

Photography began with the *camera obscura*. The Latin words mean "dark room." A camera obscura could be a box or a whole room. It had a small hole on one side. Light, reflected off an object, shone through the hole. The reflected light fell on a screen or a sheet of paper. When the light hit the screen, it made an inverted, or upside-down, picture of the object.

Camera Obscura

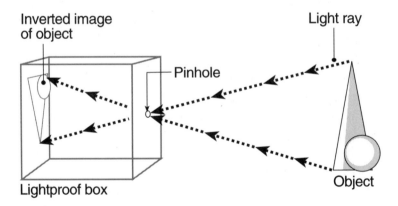

Inverted image of object

Light ray

Pinhole

Lightproof box

Object

Artists in the 1500s used the camera obscura. They projected a scene onto a piece of paper. Then they traced the image that the light made. Later, they would add details and colors to the image.

Some artists put a glass lens in the hole. A lens is a piece of glass that focuses light. The lens made the image clearer. However, these early "cameras" could not make a lasting record of an image.

Captured Moments

In the early 1800s, inventors tried to make captured images more lasting. They placed a plate of chemicals inside the camera obscura. Then they shone the light onto the plate. Light changed the chemicals. A lasting picture formed. Photography was born.

This photograph was taken in a photography studio in the 1840s.

Early cameras could make only one copy of an image. Photographers printed the image on glass or metal plates. There was no way to make more copies of the image.

Even so, the new invention was a huge success. In the past, only wealthy people had portraits of their families, which were painted by famous artists. Now, ordinary people could hang family photos in their homes.

Photography studios opened in cities and towns. People lined up by the hundreds. Often, they had to sit perfectly still for 20 minutes to get a clear photograph.

Photography quickly improved. **Negatives** and film were invented. Soon, photographers were carrying their cameras everywhere. They took pictures of Native Americans in the West. They photographed the wonders

The daily life of Civil War soldiers was captured in this early photograph.

of Europe, Africa, and Asia. They even captured the horrors of the Civil War on film.

Photographs opened up the world for many people. For the first time, they could see faraway places without ever leaving home.

Say It with Pictures

George Eastman brought cameras to ordinary people. In 1888, he sold a box camera that was loaded with film. The camera could take 100 pictures. After taking the pictures, the customer sent the camera back to the factory. There, workers developed the film and reloaded the camera. "You press the button, we do the rest," Eastman's ads explained.

Photography soon became a billion-dollar business. It was also the world's most popular hobby. By 1900, newspapers were printing photographs. Reporters traveled the world with cameras. They sent home countless images. These allowed readers at home to see the major events of the day that were happening all over the world.

At home, photographs captured every part of U.S. life. Families recorded big events and small. Cameras also helped artists to express themselves. Photography became an art form. Many photographs became as well known as famous paintings.

Using the camera, professional photographer Dorothea Lange recorded scenes of people's hard lives during the 1930s.

Moving Pictures

As cameras improved, some artists took rapid series of photographs. They wanted to study how people and animals moved. If you flipped through a stack of these photos, the pictures seemed to move.

These "moving pictures" interested Thomas Edison. He built a **kinetoscope**. It was a large wooden box. A viewer peeked into it through an eyepiece. Inside, a series of pictures moved across a lamp.

Only one person at a time could use a kinetoscope. Then, in 1895, two men in France had an idea. What if they projected the moving pictures onto a large screen? Then many people could watch the images at the same time. They built the first movie

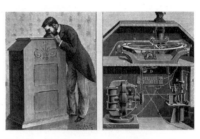

By the 1880s, people enjoyed kinetoscopes in stores and amusement parks.

projector. One night that year, they showed the first films to an audience.

These first films were not very exciting. One, for example, showed workers leaving a factory. Another showed a train pulling into a station. That one made the audience jump up and scream. They thought the train was going to hit them!

For a while, people would pay to see any "moving pictures." Soon, however, people wanted more. They wanted the pictures to tell a story. So moviemakers made hundreds of short films. The films were only 10–15 minutes long.

In the United States, the new movies were shown in **nickelodeons**. The United States had 10,000 of these theaters in 1910. Usually, a nickelodeon was an old store. It was filled with folding chairs. A large canvas screen hung in front of the room. The cost of a ticket was one nickel.

Early movies were black-and-white images with no sound. They were often disappointing. Real life, after all, had color and sound. People wanted movies to be more true to life.

Dozens of inventors worked to make movies better. In 1928, the first movie with sound was shown. The audience could finally hear the actors talk. It was a huge success. Soon, all movies were "talkies."

The 1939 film *The Wizard of Oz* shows the power of color in film. The movie begins in black and white. Then, suddenly, it shifts to full color. People loved it.

By the end of the 1930s, 85 million Americans were attending the movies every week. Movie stars were

From the 1930s on, people in the United States have enjoyed going to the movies. Movies help people learn about the different cultures of the world.

more famous than the nation's leaders. Movies influenced people's ideas and attitudes. People around the world saw the U.S. way of life on film.

The Video Age

Soon, people could buy their own movie cameras and make their own "home movies." Movie film was expensive, though. Getting enough light was a problem, too. Then, in the 1970s, **video cameras** became available. By the 1990s, many ordinary people could afford to make their own home videos.

Video cameras are easy to use. Users can watch their movies as soon as they record them. Video cameras record light as tiny electrical signals. The signals are stored as magnetic patches on videotape.

To play their videotapes, people needed **VCRs**, or **videocassette recorders**. The first ones went on sale in 1975. Before long, Hollywood movies were available on videocassettes. People began watching movies at home in addition to watching at the movie theaters.

Photography in the Computer Age

This is the computer age. Many people now have their own home computers. Why not invent a device that could use computers to send and receive photographs?

So the **digital camera** was invented. Like a regular camera, it takes snapshots. Instead of film, however, it uses a computer disk. After they take pictures, photographers slip the disks into their computers. Then they can view the pictures on the screen, print them out, or e-mail them to friends.

Photography is always changing. New inventions are on the way. Perhaps, someday, you will use them to capture the images of people and things that are important to you.

Invention by Accident

L.J.M. Daguerre.

In 1835, Louis Daguerre (dah GAIR) was trying to find a way to make the first photograph. The French inventor was not having much luck, though. Daguerre was trying to capture images on metal plates coated with silver. However, the images on the plates were too light. He could hardly see them.

Daguerre tried to make the images darker. Nothing worked. When he became tired of working, he put a few old plates in a cupboard. He planned to clean and reuse them later.

A few days later, Daguerre took the old plates out. What a surprise! There was a clear, strong image on each one!

Daguerre checked the cupboard. Something in it must have "developed" the pictures. On one shelf, he found a few drops of mercury. It had spilled there months earlier. The mercury had made the images stronger.

Daguerre named his silver-coated metal plate the **daguerreotype**. It made the first real photographs. For a while, it was very popular. Then other inventors found better ways to make photographs. Still, Daguerre's accident was the beginning of modern photography.

Chapter Five
Sending Instant Messages

People have always found ways to send messages. The ancient Chinese lit bonfires along the Great Wall. That way, people knew when an enemy was coming. Africans "talked" to their neighbors by using drums. Native Americans used smoke signals. The ancient Romans flashed mirrors.

However, there were problems with these ways of sending messages. The receiver of the message had to be close enough to see or hear the sender. The message had to be short and simple.

Native Americans used smoke signals to send messages.

Words and Wires

In the 1800s, people were putting electricity to work. By 1830, they learned that they could send electric signals over wires. All they needed was an on-off switch.

In 1844, Samuel Morse used electricity to make a new machine for sending messages. He called it the **telegraph**. (The word *telegraph* means "distance writing.")

Morse also invented a code for sending messages by telegraph. The code used a different series of short clicks and long clicks for each letter of the alphabet. Morse called the short clicks "dots." He called the long clicks "dashes."

With this Morse code, a person could tap out a message with a simple switch. The taps moved over a wire as bits of electricity.

Morse Code Symbols

Letter	Symbol	Letter	Symbol	Digit	Symbol
A	.-	N	-.	0	-----
B	-...	O	---	1	.----
C	-.-.	P	.--.	2	..---
D	-..	Q	--.-	3	...--
E	.	R	.-.	4	....-
F	..-.	S	...	5	.....
G	--.	T	-	6	-....
H	....	U	..-	7	--...
I	..	V	...-	8	---..
J	.---	W	.--	9	----.
K	-.-	X	-..-		
L	.-..	Y	-.--		
M	--	Z	--..		

To send a telegram, operators used a machine like this to spell out a message in dots and dashes.

With the telegraph, people could send messages quickly. Before the telegraph, it took weeks to receive news from distant places. Now, people could get news in hours.

Businesses also liked the speed of the telegraph. Before the telegraph, a business letter might take weeks to reach someone. A **telegram**, a message sent by telegraph, arrived in just hours.

By 1861, telegraph wires ran from New York City to San Francisco. The telegraph also became a tool of war. Both sides in the Civil War put up telegraph poles. They strung miles of wire. With the telegraph, generals could keep in touch with their troops.

By 1883, the United States had 400,000 miles of telegraph wires. Millions of messages hummed along the lines. The railroads loved the telegraph. Workers in train stations could now pass on important messages to other stations. As a result, the trains ran more smoothly than ever.

Voices Over Wires

The telegraph gave people a new dream. What if electric signals could copy a human voice? Then people could speak to friends in other cities as if they were in the same room!

In 1876, Alexander Graham Bell made the dream come true. Bell was a teacher of deaf students, those who cannot hear. He knew about the science of voices and other sounds.

Bell built a simple machine that changed sounds into electric signals. These signals flashed along a wire. They moved about one million times faster than the speed of sound. At the other end of the wire, another machine changed the signals back to sounds.

The telephone was an instant success. People in distant places could now talk to each other from their own homes. It was much easier to use than the telegraph. It was also more private.

By 1900, the United States had more than a million telephones. By 1910, the number jumped to 7.6 million. The telephone also created new jobs. Workers put up telephone wires and repaired them. Operators helped connect the telephone calls. Between 1876 and 1976, three million Americans found work in telephone companies.

With the telephone, people could speak directly to faraway friends and family members.

Today, the world has more than a billion phones. We use them for shopping, doing business, getting information, and chatting. Phone lines carry signals from computers and fax machines. They help people around the globe to communicate instantly.

Now, many people even have phones in their cars. By the 1990s, people were carrying tiny **cellular phones**, which are small wireless telephones. Everywhere they went, they could now send or receive phone messages. The telephone plays a larger part in our lives than ever!

Voices Across the World

The air around you is filled with **radio waves**. They carry music and all the latest news. You cannot see or feel these waves. With a radio, though, you can hear them.

Many people helped to create the radio. By the 1800s, scientists knew that an **electric current** in one wire could create a current in another wire. This happened even when the wires were not connected.

Why does this happen? Electric current creates radio waves in the air. These waves travel through the air at the speed of light. When the waves reach another wire, they turn back into electricity.

In 1895, an Italian inventor put these radio waves to work. Guglielmo Marconi built the first **radio**. He used it to send signals without using any wires.

At first, ships were the major users of the radio. Sailors could send important signals to other ships or to people on shore by radio.

Soon, people found ways to send voice messages by radio. Small radio stations popped up around the United States. These stations could send through the air, or **broadcast**, the same message to everyone who had a radio.

In 1920, one radio station broadcast the results of an election. Another station created the first sports broadcast. It was a live report from a World Series baseball game. Once again, the speed of sending news had increased. The radio could instantly connect millions of listeners.

Families gathered around their radios to hear important news or their favorite programs.

The Golden Age of Radio

The Golden Age of radio began in 1925. Children rushed home from school to hear their favorite shows. Families gathered around to listen to comedy shows, plays, and music. People could now sit in their living rooms and hear famous singers and actors.

People also turned to the radio for news. President Franklin D. Roosevelt used the radio to bring the nation together. During the 1930s and 1940s, he gave many radio talks. He called them "fireside chats."

Pictures in the Air

Sounds could travel by radio waves. Could pictures do the same thing? A man named John Baird wanted to find out. In 1925, he built a strange machine in his attic. He built it from an old tea box, bicycle lights, sewing needles, and string.

One day, Baird asked a young neighbor to walk in front of his big box. The boy was the first person ever to be on television!

By 1928, Baird could send television pictures across the Atlantic Ocean. The quality of the pictures was not very good, though. So other people built an improved television. It sent much clearer pictures.

In 1936, a New York City station became the first to broadcast television programs. At that time, only 150 homes in the United States had TVs. The first show was a cartoon, *Felix the Cat.*

After World War II (1941–1945), television became popular. By 1950, about four million American households owned TVs. By 1960, nearly nine out of every ten American families owned at least one television set.

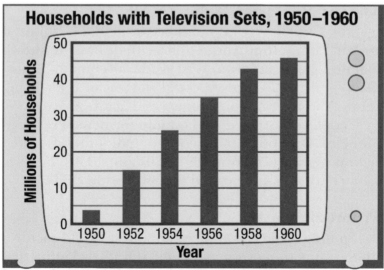

Source: *Statistical Abstract of the United States*

By the 1960s, television reached more people than any other form of communication. Many Americans began spending their free time in front of the TV. Parents worried about TV's effects on their children. People worried that viewers were spending too much time at home and were becoming "couch potatoes."

However, television also brought the world closer together. TV viewers could instantly see what was going on all over the world. In the 1960s and 1970s, television brought scenes from the Vietnam War into people's living rooms. It made people face the serious impact of war. The Olympic games were broadcast to every corner of the world, linking millions of viewers. Today, people around the world can see important events as they happen. Television has made the entire world a global village.

The First TV Broadcasts

Television has come a long way! In 1932, a New York City station began the first TV broadcasts. The broadcasters were not sure how far the images would travel. They didn't know if the images would be clear.

Only a few Americans had TV sets in 1932. No newspapers printed TV schedules. So early viewers just hunted around the dial to find a picture. When they did, they often wrote to the TV station.

"I have been looking in on your station for 6 months," a Tennessee man wrote. "Often, someone is playing a violin. I have noticed a ring on his finger."

That was big news. The next day, *The New York Times* ran the story with this headline: "Ring on Violinist's Finger Seen in Tennessee."

Some viewers wrote to check on what they had seen. "We saw several pictures last night," a Vermont woman wrote. "The first was a man. The two others were women. Were they different women?"

Others wrote with suggestions. "All TV performers should wear white," wrote one. "That way, they are easier to see."

"Television has its problems," the director of the station noted. "In time, however, things will get better."

Chapter Six
Going Online

We think of the computer as a modern tool. The idea for this invention, however, is more than 100 years old. In 1834, an Englishman named Charles Babbage designed the first computer. It was as big as a bus. Babbage's machine could store and find information. To do so, it used cards with holes punched through them.

Babbage spent 40 years trying to build his computer. He never finished. He did not have enough money, and no one would lend him any. Back then, people thought computers would never be useful.

Early computers were huge. They used ideas developed by Charles Babbage in the 1830s.

In 1943, the British built the first computer. They called it Colossus. They used it to break enemy codes. Colossus helped the Allies to win World War II.

In 1946, the United States built an all-purpose computer. Its name was ENIAC. The monster machine filled a huge room at the University of Pennsylvania. ENIAC had more than 19,000 electronic tubes.

In the 1960s and 1970s, computers were large and very expensive. However, they became common in government offices and large companies. Computers helped people do some jobs much faster. Scientists used computers to store information and to do complex math problems.

Early computers were not nearly as fast or as powerful as today's machines. In 1969, for example, NASA used many computers to send astronauts to the moon. All of its computers together had about as much power as one of today's personal computers!

Early computers, such as this, stored information on paper cards and magnetic tape.

Personal Computing

Microchips, or integrated circuits, were invented in 1959. These tiny chips integrated, or combined, many different computer parts into one circuit. A **circuit** is the path of an electric current.

With microchips, computers became smaller and cheaper. Home computers became a possibility. However, many thought there was no need for such an invention. What would ordinary people do with computers?

The first personal computer went on sale in 1975. This little black box was not "user friendly." There was no keyboard and no screen. Customers had to build it themselves from a kit. It was not a big success.

Three years later, two young men in California were busy in their garage. There, they built the first successful personal computer. Steve Jobs and Steve Wozniak called their computer the Apple. It had a color screen and a keyboard like the ones on today's computers.

Steve Jobs and Steve Wozniak worked on a machine that would become the first successful home computer, the Apple.

During the 1980s, the number of personal computers grew rapidly. Ordinary people found many uses for their home computers. Some people used them to play games or manage money. Others used them to write letters and reports. Some people even created computer art.

People also plugged their computers into their telephone lines. That opened up a whole new world of communication—the **Internet**.

Inventing the Internet

In 1969, four scientists linked their computers. They all worked for the Defense Department of the U.S. government. The linkup made sharing information easier. A note written on one computer could be sent to all the others. The scientists called their computer link a **network**.

In 1984, the National Science Foundation started its own network. The purpose was to share scientific information. Some businesses and colleges became part of the network.

This system of linked computers grew slowly at first. By 1985, there were about 5,000 users. Most of them were scientists. Then other groups began forming computer networks, too. Soon, the networks became interconnected. Users called this system an Inter-Net-Network. Today, we just call it the Internet.

Soon, ordinary people learned about the Internet. They thought it had a lot to offer them, too. The Internet quickly became popular. By 1995, more than 50 million people were using it. Today, the Internet is huge. About one million new users go **online** every month to get connected to the Internet.

The Internet System

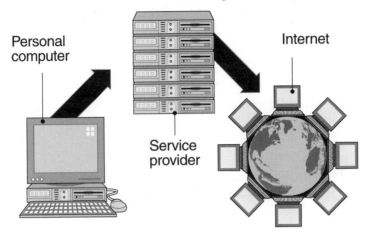

Personal computer

Service provider

Internet

Communicating on the Internet

Today, the Internet has many different parts. They were invented or developed by many people. All of these parts fit together. There are many parts of the Internet that help people communicate.

The **World Wide Web** was created in 1992. It is probably the most popular piece of the Internet. Companies, organizations, and individuals have **Web sites**, or Web pages, on the World Wide Web. Once online, you can jump from one page to another. You can read information, view pictures, listen to sounds, and buy products. You can even experience whitewater rafting or blasting off in the space shuttle.

E-mail is the oldest part of the Internet. (The *e* stands for "electronic.") The first e-mail was sent in the early 1970s. E-mail is simply a way to write a letter on one computer and send it to another.

You can e-mail a letter to your friend down the street. You can also e-mail a friend who lives thousands of miles away. The letters arrive in the receivers' electronic mailboxes almost immediately.

Usenet newsgroups are like huge bulletin boards, each devoted to a particular topic. People all over the world can read and post messages on these bulletin boards. You can express your ideas and feelings about a favorite sports team, music group, or TV show. You can discuss history, math, and science. There is probably a newsgroup for any topic that interests you.

Chat is another way to communicate on the Internet. Online chatrooms are like meeting halls. A group of people at a chatroom site can talk about anything. People from all over the United States—and the world—can share their views.

Bringing It All Together

The computer brings together many forms of communication. For example, almost everyone writes with computers today. Word processing programs make writing and editing easier than ever.

Writers also use computers to do research on the Internet. Trips to the library are less necessary. Of course, there will always be books. More and more people, however, are finding information online. They can also **download** information from the Internet. When people download material, they are actually receiving a computer file from another computer.

The computer also makes it possible for people to design and print their own books in their own homes. People can even "publish" their books on the Internet and reach millions of readers.

Computers use the latest advances in sound recording, too. Most computers now have speakers. People can play their favorite CDs on computers. In addition, many Web pages come alive with sound.

The computer brings together many forms of communication, such as words, sounds, and images.

Images are a big part of computers, too. Digital cameras make it easy to edit and e-mail photos. A digital camera records images on a computer disk instead of on film.

Many Web sites have video images. You can see and hear the action on your computer screen. Rather than visit the video store, some people even download movies to their computers.

What Does the Future Hold?

It is not easy to predict what will happen next in the computer age. Things are happening too fast! Whatever happens, computers will play a big role.

Computers will become less expensive. They will also get smaller. In the future, people may wear tiny computers on their wrists. They will use them to send e-mail. They will use them to explore the Internet.

At some point, computer chips will be no bigger than the head of a pin. One of these chips might hold all recorded knowledge. You could wear it in your watch, for example. If you had a question, you would just say it aloud. You would get an answer on the spot.

Computers may also drive the cars of the future. Drivers would just say where they want to go, and the car would do the rest. With computers doing the driving, there might be fewer accidents. People would have time to do other things while traveling. Computer-driven flying cars are another possibility. They might make traffic jams a thing of the past.

Does this vision of the future seem hard to believe? Try to keep an open mind. Remember that it took just 75 years to advance from the Wright brothers' airplane to the space shuttle. Since then, the pace of new inventions has sped up. Inventors still have the power to change our lives!

Expressing Yourself on the Internet

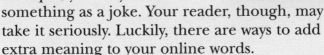

When you write an e-mail or "talk" in a chatroom, readers cannot see your face, your hands, or your body language. This can lead to misunderstandings. For example, you may write something as a joke. Your reader, though, may take it seriously. Luckily, there are ways to add extra meaning to your online words.

Many people use special keyboard symbols called "emoticons" to show how they feel. The word *emoticon* is a blend of the words *emotion* and *icon*. The most commonly used emoticon is the smiley face.

Here are some emoticons you can use:

:-)   a smile
;-)   a smile and a wink
;->   a wink and a big grin
:-(a frown

If you really want to make a point, YOU CAN SHOUT IT OUT! On the Internet, shouting means typing in capital letters. Don't shout too often, though. Your readers will find it annoying.

Internet users also type special initials to show how they are feeling. For example, the initials *lol* mean that the writer is "laughing out loud."

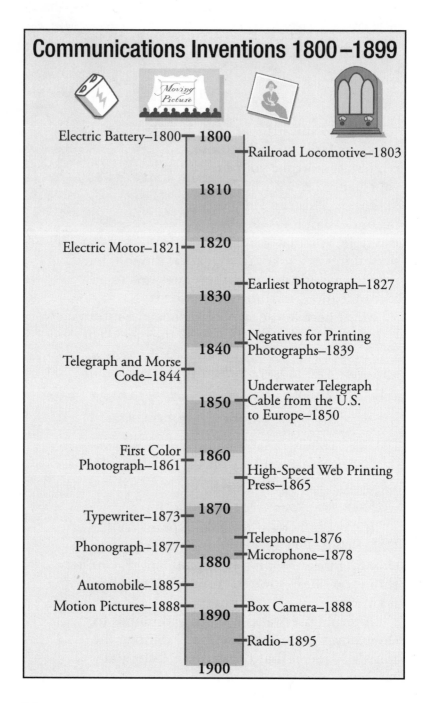

Communications Inventions 1800–1899

Electric Battery–1800 — **1800**

Railroad Locomotive–1803

1810

Electric Motor–1821 — **1820**

Earliest Photograph–1827

1830

Negatives for Printing
Photographs–1839

1840

Telegraph and Morse
Code–1844

Underwater Telegraph
Cable from the U.S.
to Europe–1850

1850

First Color
Photograph–1861 — **1860**

High-Speed Web Printing
Press–1865

Typewriter–1873 — **1870**

Telephone–1876

Phonograph–1877 — Microphone–1878

1880

Automobile–1885 —

Motion Pictures–1888 — **1890** — Box Camera–1888

Radio–1895

1900

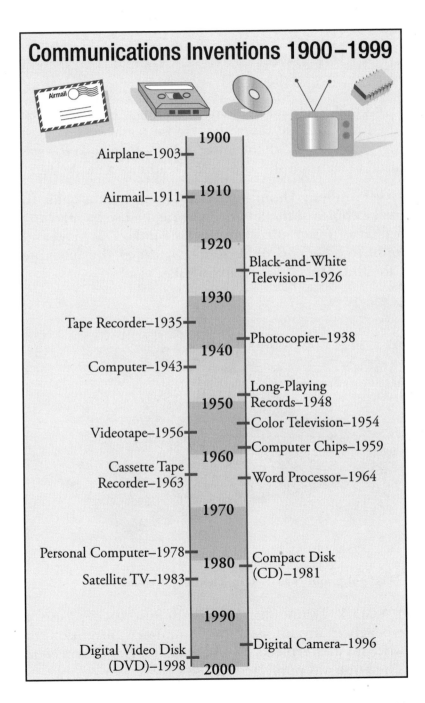

Communications Inventions 1900–1999

1900

Airplane–1903

1910

Airmail–1911

1920

Black-and-White Television–1926

1930

Tape Recorder–1935

Photocopier–1938

1940

Computer–1943

Long-Playing Records–1948

1950

Color Television–1954

Videotape–1956

Computer Chips–1959

1960

Cassette Tape Recorder–1963

Word Processor–1964

1970

Personal Computer–1978

1980

Compact Disk (CD)–1981

Satellite TV–1983

1990

Digital Camera–1996

Digital Video Disk (DVD)–1998

2000

55

Fascinating Facts About Communications Inventions

■ Quills are pens made from feathers. They were first used about 2,500 years ago. Goose feathers were best because they held the most ink. A special knife was used to sharpen the end of the feather—a penknife.

■ President Thomas Jefferson wrote with a quill. To make copies of the letters he wrote, he used a machine called a "polygraph." The machine linked his hand and quill to a second quill. Jefferson called the machine "the finest invention of the present age."

This "polygraph" was used by Thomas Jefferson.

■ Mark Twain was the first author to ever use a typewriter. Twain used the brand-new invention to write his masterpiece, *The Adventures of Huckleberry Finn.* The book was published in 1884.

- Alexander Graham Bell first spoke on the telephone by accident. He was setting up a test phone when he spilled some acid. "Mr. Watson, come here; I want you!" he called to his helper. In the next room, his helper heard the words over the phone. So the first phone call was actually a call for help!

- The first battery-powered hearing aid was invented in 1923. It came in a large case that weighed more than 16 pounds! By 1935, the hearing aid had become much smaller. Still, it weighed $2\frac{1}{2}$ pounds. Today, with transistors, hearing aids are almost weightless.

- In 1910, a murderer escaped from England on a ship that was on its way to the United States. He might have gotten away, but the ship was carrying a new invention—a radio. English police sent a message to the ship in midocean. Since then, the police have caught many criminals using their radios.

Radio communication has made it easier for the police to catch criminals.

Donna Auguste holds her invention, the Newton Computer.

■ In 1993, Donna Auguste, an engineer at The Apple Computer Company, led the team that created the Newton. The Newton was one of the first handheld computers.

■ Bette Graham was a typist in the 1950s. Back then, a person had to retype a letter if there were any mistakes. Rather than do that, Graham mixed up a tiny bottle of white paint. She hid it in her desk and secretly painted over her mistakes. This was the beginning of Liquid Paper. Soon, word of her invention got out. By the 1970s, Graham had a company worth $50 million!

■ Some wasps build nests of paper. They chew twigs to make the paper. Almost 300 years ago, a French scientist studied the juices in a wasp's stomach. Based on what he learned, modern papermaking became possible.

■ The ballpoint pen was invented in 1938. Pilots in World War II (1941–1945) liked the pens. Ballpoints never leaked, even at high altitudes. The pens also wrote underwater.

■ By the 1890s, many homes had telephones. Telephone owners often put on good clothes and combed their hair before making a call. They seemed to think the person on the other end of the line could see them!

■ Charles Babbage designed computers in the 1830s. He was never able to build one, though. In 1991, engineers in London, England, studied Babbage's designs. They decided to build one based on his designs. Guess what? The machine worked!

Charles Babbage's designs paved the way for modern computers.

GLOSSARY

broadcast (BRAHD kast)
to send sounds or images through the air using radio waves that can be received by radios or television sets (40)

cassette tape (kə SET TAYP)
a type of small magnetic tape used for recording and playing back sound (25)

cellular phone (SEL yə lar FOHN)
a small wireless telephone that receives radio waves (39)

circuit (SER kit)
a path of an electric current (47)

communicate (kə MYOO nə KAYT)
to send information, thoughts, ideas, or feelings from one person to another (4)

compact disk (KAHM pakt DISK)
a small, plastic-coated metal disk on which sound has been recorded; the sound is read by a laser beam (25)

cylinder (SIL ən dər)
a tube; many early materials for recording sound were cylinders (20)

daguerreotype (də GER ə TEYEP)
an early type of photograph that fixed an image on a metal plate (34)

digital camera (DIJ ə təl KAM ə rə)
a camera that records images onto a computer disk (33)

download (DOUN LOHD)
to transfer data from one computer to another (50)

electric current (i LEK trik KER ənt)
the flow of electrons through a wire (40)

e-mail (EE MAYL)
electronic mail sent from one computer to another (49)

Internet (IN tər net)
a system of interconnected computer networks that link computers around the world and allow them to share information (48)

invention (in VEN shən)
a new idea or machine (4)

kinetoscope (kə NET ə SKOHP)
an early invention for viewing motion pictures (31)

loudspeaker (LOUD SPEE kər)
device for changing electricity to sounds and amplifying them (22)

magnetic tape (mag NET ik TAYP)
a type of tape on which sound can be recorded (23)

microchip (MEYE kroh CHIP)
a tiny chip that combines many different computer parts into one circuit (47)

microphone (MEYE krə FOHN)
a device for changing sound waves into an electric current (21)

negative (NEG ə tiv)
in photography, a piece of film with light and dark reversed (28)

network (NET WERK)
a group of computers joined by links that carry information (48)

nickelodeon (nik ə LOH dee ən)
a place where the first motion pictures were shown; the admission charge was five cents (31)

online (AHN LEYEN)
being connected to another computer system (48)

papyrus (pə PEYE rus)
a plant used by ancient Egyptians to make paper (5)

parchment (PAHRCH mənt)
a writing material made from animal skins (6)

phonograph (FOH nə GRAF)
an early machine for playing sound recordings (20)

photography (fə TAHG rə fee)
the process of capturing images on metal, glass, or paper (27)

printing press (PRINT ing PRES)
a machine for printing from movable type (8)

projector (prə JEK tər)
a machine for placing an image or movie on a screen for viewing (31)

radio (RAY dee oh)
a device that changes radio waves to electricity and then changes the electricity to sound (40)

radio waves (RAY dee oh WAYVZ)
a type of radiation that travels through the air at the speed of light (40)

record (ri KORD)
to store sound so that people can listen to it at another time or place (20)

record (REK ərd)

a plastic disk, available in different sizes, that is used for recording sound; it is less commonly used now, since the invention of cassettes and compact disks (21)

stagecoach (STAYJ KOHCH)

a large, wheeled vehicle, pulled by horses, that carried passengers in the 1700s and 1800s (12)

steam engine (STEEM EN jən)

an engine operated by steam; usually a sliding piston in a cylinder is moved by the expansion of the steam (14)

tape recorder (TAYP ri KORD ər)

a machine for recording sound onto magnetic tape (23)

telegram (TEL ə GRAM)

a message sent by telegraph (37)

telegraph (TEL ə GRAF)

a system of sending coded messages over a wire with electrical impulses (36)

transportation (tranz pər TAY shən)

any means of carrying people or goods from one place to another (12)

type (TEYEP)

a piece of metal with a raised letter on one side; type can be moved to print words (8)

Usenet (YOOZ NET)

an Internet-based discussion system that uses bulletin boards on which people can post questions, news, and comments about specific topics (50)

vehicle (VEE ə kəl)

anything that carries people or goods from place to place (12)

video camera (VID ee oh KAM ə rə)

a camera that records images and sounds on videotape (33)

videocassette recorder (VID ee oh kə SET ri KORD ər) **(VCR)**

a device that can record events, movies, or television programs onto videotape and can play back videotape so that it can be viewed on a television screen (33)

Web site

a specific location on the World Wide Web, also called a Web page (49)

World Wide Web

a part of the Internet that allows individuals, companies, and organizations to share information (49)

INDEX

Photo Credits